Tintagel Castle

Colleen E Batey

Introduction

Built half on the mainland and half on a jagged headland projecting into the Cornish sea, Tintagel Castle is one of the most spectacular historic sites in Britain. Its association with King Arthur makes it also one of the most famous, but the history of the site stretches back centuries before the first tales of Arthur.

During the so-called Dark Ages (roughly the fifth to the seventh centuries) Tintagel was an important stronghold. Large quantities of pottery fragments – remains of luxury goods imported from the Mediterranean – were left behind by those who lived here. In its highly defensible position it is likely to have been a residence of a Dark-Age ruler of Cornwall.

Tintagel emerges again in the 12th century – but as legend, not history – as a seat of Cornish kings in Geoffrey of Monmouth's *History of the Kings of Britain* (c.1138), and in Continental poems telling the story of Tristan and Yseult. The remains visible today belong to a castle built a hundred years later on the orders of the hugely rich and ambitious Richard (1209–72), earl of Cornwall. The site was of no strategic value; legend alone seems to have inspired Richard to build in this place.

Although the castle had fallen into disrepair by the 1330s, its mythical associations meant that it remained a source of interest. Tourists were arriving by the end of the 17th century, and during the 19th century the explosion of interest in Arthurian legend and the expansion of the railway brought vast numbers to the site.

In the 1930s the archaeologist Ralegh Radford uncovered remains on the Island of what he thought was an early Christian monastery. Archaeological discoveries since have suggested otherwise, but in many ways Tintagel's early history remains mysterious. Together with its spectacular landscape, its mystery has helped to foster the site's special significance, as a place of legend long associated with King Arthur.

Above: King Arthur, as imagined in this photograph of 1874 by Julia Margaret Cameron

Facing page: The remains of Tintagel's northern ruins catching the last light of the setting sun

Tour of Tintagel

The appearance of the headland has
changed dramatically over time. Centuries
of landslips have taken many parts of the
castle and earlier buildings with them.
When building began on the castle in the
late 1230s, it straddled a short neck of
land, or isthmus. This section of the castle
has now fallen into the sea, so that the
remains are in two separate parts, linked
by the present, much diminished, neck
of rock spanned by a wooden bridge.
The original entrance to the castle, and
to the upper and lower courtyards, is
on the mainland; the inner courtyard
containing the principal castle buildings
is on the peninsula known as the Island.

FOLLOWING THE TOUR

*The guidebook tour starts at the ticket booth by the great ditch
and takes in the mainland courtyards before moving over the
bridge to the Island. Many visitors approach the starting point
via the Visitor Centre at the bottom of the valley, either taking
the path to the bridge and the steps up to the left, or climbing
the gentler zig-zag footpath from the Visitor Centre up the side
of the valley; others choose to tour the Island before returning
to tour the mainland. The small numbered plans in the margins
highlight the key points of the tour.*

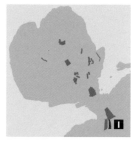

Left: Part of the great ditch, with the remains of the lower courtyard's 13th-century curtain wall beyond

Below left: At the time of Richard of Cornwall the gate tower guarded access to the castle, as is shown in this reconstruction drawing. Richard is shown on horseback inside the inner mainland courtyard

Below: The remains of the gate tower today, seen from the south

Facing page: An aerial view of Tintagel, showing the ruins of the castle stretching from the mainland across to the Island

◼ APPROACH TO THE CASTLE

The approach to the castle is from the south, through the ruins of an outer gateway. Ahead and to the left, on the high crag, are the remains of the curtain walls of the mainland courtyards and of the gate tower straight ahead along the path.

To the right of the path is the great ditch. Near this defensive ditch a purse of late Roman coins was found in 1955, but the ditch itself was cut or modified from a natural feature in the landscape during the Dark Ages. The earth and rock were piled up to form a steep bank, and a stone wall or timber palisade was probably built on top of it.

When Richard, earl of Cornwall, brother of Henry III, acquired Tintagel between 1233 and 1236, any buildings were likely to have long disintegrated or been overgrown with grass. The great ditch would have been the most prominent altered feature of the landscape. Richard probably had the ditch recut, and had a stone wall built on top of the bank to form the main entrance to his castle.

The curtain walls visible on approaching, and the ruins of the gate tower, date from the time of Richard. Keepers of the gate tower controlled entry into the mainland courtyards. The tower would have been closed by a great wooden door, locked by a timber bar. When the door was opened, the bar was drawn back along the stone channel visible at the back of the gate tower's wall.

At the foot of the entrance to the gate tower can be seen the only surviving dressed stones on the site. The gate tower had a chamber above the entrance. Probably shortly after the castle was built the gate tower was strengthened by buttresses at the back and on the lower side.

Late in the 14th century, after the castle had fallen into disrepair, two flanking towers were built outside the north-east curtain wall on the slope of the ditch.

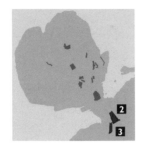

▣ LOWER MAINLAND COURTYARD

Through the gate is the castle's lower courtyard. It is smaller than in Richard's time, as parts of it to the west and north have fallen into the sea. On the north-east and south-east sides it was enclosed by a curtain wall 1.5m thick. The outside would have been rendered and possibly lime-washed, making the castle appear dazzling white against the landscape. Various types of local stone were used: slates and 'greenstones' (volcanic tuff and hard epidiorite). Epidiorite was used for decorative features such as mouldings, and although these are now worn or missing, having fallen into the ditch in some cases, they would have made a dramatic contrast against the whitewashed walls. The rectangular holes that can be seen in the walls supported timber scaffolding during the construction of the castle.

There would have been buildings, probably timber, elsewhere in the courtyard, for storage and stabling horses. A small room on the right of the gate probably housed the porter or entry guard. The door jambs were cut to hold a wooden frame. At the far end of the room the wall is carried across the stair that originally gave access to the wall-walk from the gate. The stair must have been ruinous by the time this far wall was built, probably in the 15th century. On the north-east of the courtyard is the base of a double stairway leading to the wall-walk remains.

Dark-Age Remains

The remains of any buildings from this period lie deep under the later medieval deposits, destroyed or buried when the ground was levelled to make the courtyard. Traces of metalworking have been found from this time, and pottery from as early as the fifth century, as well as two exciting finds of glass. One glass sherd belonged to a large dish that seems to have been decorated with a pattern of scrolls and circles, or possibly lettering.

The luxurious imported goods found here, including this dish, provide evidence that the site was used by a series of rich and locally powerful people, perhaps the rulers of Cornwall, over a period of about 200 years from the fifth century.

▣ UPPER MAINLAND COURTYARD

To the left of the entrance to the lower courtyard, steps cut into the cliff led to the gate tower. From here there was access to the wall-walk and upper courtyard. The steps have been reconstructed.

The upper courtyard is a long narrow area sloping up to the south. Like the lower courtyard, it encompassed a much larger area before erosion. The east side is enclosed by a curtain wall, dating from the 13th century, which curves round and ends abruptly at the cliff edge. It had a parapet and wall-walk, approached by a stairway, the remains of which can be seen in the centre of this stretch of the wall.

Above: A king directs the building of a castle, in this illustration from a 15th-century copy of Geoffrey of Monmouth's History of the Kings of Britain. *The castle seems to be being built on a projecting headland, as was Tintagel*

Right: The mainland courtyards seen from the north, with Tintagel parish church behind the rise

The cliff marks the limits of the south-western wall. Where the precipice falls sheer on the western side was a landfall in the Middle Ages, when part of the cliff and part of the courtyard with it collapsed into the sea. The straight wall at the edge was built afterwards, probably in the late 14th century, and was once the same height as the other walls. It too is now falling away at its north end. The cliff was not only an excellent defensive feature but also enabled the efficient removal of waste: the two projections from this wall were latrines opening over the cliff. The one to the north was enclosed in a small tower which projected from the wall. Nearby are the remains of a stairway that led up to the roof of the tower.

By the steps to the lower courtyard is a series of small rooms dating from the late 14th or 15th century. The stone door jambs are cut with a slot to hold wooden door frames. They may have been built after the landfall to replace buildings lost in the collapse and would possibly have formed the lodgings of a guard.

Dark-Age Remains

The low grass-covered walls at the north end of the courtyard are founded on a different level from the castle buildings. Fragments of imported pottery from the Dark Ages were found nearby, suggesting that these buildings were part of the earlier stronghold. Like most of the remains thought to date from the Dark Ages seen on the site, they were reconstructed in the 1930s by Ralegh Radford's team. It is possible that these buildings were re-used as temporary dwellings when Earl Richard built the castle. The lower layers of stone of the massive, curved enclosing wall may have been part of the Dark-Age defences of this crag.

Key to the mainland courtyards seen from the south-east:

A Upper mainland courtyard

B Lower mainland courtyard

C Great ditch

D Curtain wall

E Outer gate

F Inner gate and gate tower

G Porter's lodge (probable)

H Stairway

I Double stairway (to wall-walk)

J Latrine

c.1260

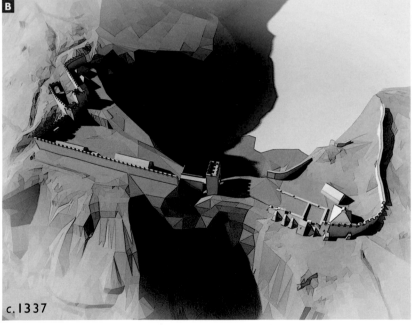

c.1337

A *Richard of Cornwall built his castle over the mainland and the Island, the courtyards linked by a gate with a drawbridge*

B *By 1337 part of the Great Hall of the Island courtyard and the west wall of the mainland courtyard had fallen into the sea*

BRIDGE

During the fifth and sixth centuries, an isthmus would have enabled passage directly from the far (north-western) end of the lower courtyard to the Island. This isthmus survived into the 12th century, as recorded by the scholar Geoffrey of Monmouth (d.1154/5) in his *History of the Kings of Britain*, who writes that the only entrance to the Island stronghold 'in the sea and shut in on all sides by it' was by a narrow rock that 'three armed soldiers would be able to defend, even if you had the whole kingdom of Britain at your side'.

This narrow approach to the Island possibly gave the stronghold its name, from the Cornish *din* or *tin*, meaning a fortress or a natural stronghold resembling a fortress, and *tagell*, meaning a constriction: Din Tagell, the Fortress of the Narrow Entrance.

By the 1230s, when Richard built his castle, the isthmus had already partly eroded. On the side of the cliff, beside the steps, rubbish deposits dating from before the building of the castle have been exposed by later landfalls. By 1540, when the poet and antiquary John Leland (c.1503–1552) visited

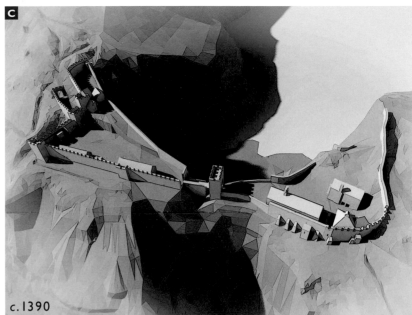

c.1390

c.1540

the site, he observed that the only way onto the Island was 'by longe elme trees layde for a bryge'. On his map of about 1604 the cartographer John Norden (c.1547–1625) labels the gap between the Island and mainland 'a draw bridge decay'd', and shows a man in a red tunic climbing the 'verie steepe and craggie' cliffs to gain passage.

Richard Byrn Kinsman, vicar of Tintagel parish from 1851 to 1894, when Tintagel was becoming a popular tourist destination, had steps cut into the cliff in the 1850s by local quarrymen to enable visitors to climb onto the Island. By the 1970s this route had become hazardous, and the present bridge was built. Some of Kinsman's unaltered steps are clearly visible on the left of the bridge, to the western side of the isthmus; the lower steps have fallen into the sea.

This western inlet is the most exposed to storms and many of the boulders on the beach below the bridge have been dislodged from the cliffs by waves and wind. In contrast, the sandy eastern inlet to the right of the bridge, known as the Haven, is a relatively sheltered bay where in more recent times slate was loaded onto boats.

C *By about 1390 the west wall of the mainland courtyard had been rebuilt, and lodgings built on the site of the Great Hall*

D *The drawbridge and gate had fallen into the sea, and the lodgings reduced in size, by about 1540*

Centre: *The bridge today between the mainland (left) and the Island (right)*

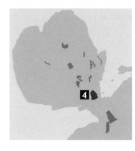

Below: Sir Lancelot at the table of Arthur and Guinevere, from La Queste del Saint Graal, c. 1300–15. During the Middle Ages noble families aspired to the chivalric values expressed in Arthurian legends

Right: The remains of the Great Hall, seen from the west. The letters correspond to the plan on the facing page

4 ISLAND COURTYARD

Access to the medieval Island courtyard, as to the mainland courtyards, was through a gate tower with a chamber above it. Now the remains of the courtyard are reached through a gate in a wall at the top of the steps. The gate tower, together with sections of the curtain wall and part of the Great Hall on the south side, has fallen into the sea, making the courtyard much smaller than it was.

When the curtain wall was built, between 1240 and 1260, it formed a high battlemented enclosure right around the courtyard. What remains of the original wall starts on the edge of the western cliff and follows the top of the steep slope overlooking the courtyard. It is better preserved on the north side, where it descends the hill in a series of steps. In 1852 the Revd Richard Kinsman strengthened and embellished this original 13th-century wall.

The coping (shaped, top layer of a wall) is his restoration. The use of native slate dressed with the hard local 'greenstone' can be seen best in the gate. Several small square holes that can be seen in the original wall held scaffolding used during its construction.

Great Hall

As originally built in the 13th century, the Great Hall was the largest and most important building of the castle – the place where Earl Richard or his ministers would dine, entertain and sleep. It was probably a single-storey building with a screens passage (a passage running across the end of the hall) dividing the main hall from the pantry and buttery at its south end, where food and drink were stored and prepared. The private apartments were probably incorporated at the north end.

Probably as a result of the cliff falls at its south end, the Great Hall fell into decay, and by 1337 it was described in a survey of the duchy of Cornwall as 'ruinous and its walls of no strength'. Its roof was dismantled and its timbers put into store at about this time on the orders of John of Eltham (d. 1336), brother of Edward III (r. 1326/7–77), and then earl of Cornwall.

By 1345 Edward (1330–76), the Black Prince, was duke of Cornwall, and had ordered repairs to the castle. A smaller building with a hall, buttery, pantry and kitchen was built within the remaining walls of the Great Hall. The kitchen was subdivided and expanded to the north, and another latrine was built through the curtain wall. Today this two-storey building is the most prominent feature visible. It was built possibly to house high-status prisoners of the Crown, who are known to have been held at Tintagel at the time, or for the resident constable, who was responsible for the security of the castle.

In the 15th century this smaller building on the site of the Great Hall was reduced in size, probably as a result of further erosion.

Western Chambers

On the upper side of the Island courtyard at the base of the cliff was a small two-storey lodging containing two rooms. The remains of both rooms have external doorways with recesses for wooden door frames (dated to the 14th century).

Key to the plan and
photograph of the
Great Hall
A Great Hall
B Reduced two-storey
house
C Two-storey house
D Latrine
E Kitchen
F Gate
G Curtain wall
H Two-storey building
(western chambers)

Large sections at the south end of Richard's original Great Hall, where the buttery and pantry stood, have completely fallen away in landslips. The remains are obscured by three subsequent building phases.

The original hall was built on a platform of made ground with a retaining wall on its east side. The lower parts of some of the hall windows survive, as do some of the recesses within the walls that held its timber roof trusses.

Probably in about 1240, a few years after building work on the castle was begun, buttresses were built against the east wall of the hall when the platform on which the hall stood began to subside. At the same time the battlemented curtain wall was built around the Island side of the inner courtyard, together with a detached kitchen north of the hall and a latrine on the east side of the hall.

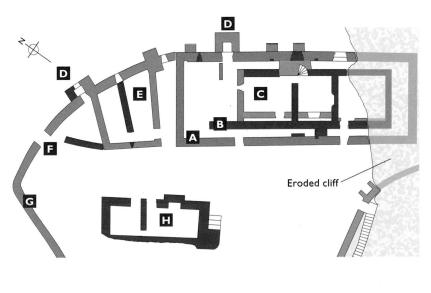

Eroded cliff

| 0 | 5metres | | c.1240 | c.1260 | c.1340 | c.1500 | Post 1852 |

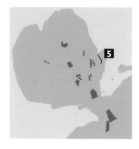

Between 1 and 2 a draw bridge decaid
Between 1 and 3 the descent
Between 3 and 2 the ascent
3 the Isthmos. 4 buildings fallen into y Sea
5 the old Chappell. 6 a spring of fresh water
7 the Iron gate. 8 a vaulte thorow y rock
9 a gate guarded with Iron at the entrance
into the first buylding on land side. 10 the
mayn buylding on the land side. 11 the
euyned buylding on the Ilunde

Right: John Norden's depiction of Tintagel of about 1604, showing the treacherous passage to the Island, and sheep grazing among the castle buildings
Below: John Leland, by Thomas Charles Wageman, after a 16th-century portrait by Hans Holbein the Younger

Facing page: The 'Iron Gate' above the rocks and cove on the east side of the Island

'Upon the North Clif is Tintagel, the which Castel had be like three Wardes, whereof two be woren away with gulfing in of the Sea, in so much that it hath made there almost an Isle.'
John Leland, c.1540

The lower part of the back wall is cut out of the rock and part of it survives in the north-west corner as a bench. The room to the south has a fireplace. On the southern side is the base of stairs that probably led to an upper storey. This small lodging may have been used by one of the officials of the castle, possibly the chaplain.

Dark-Age Remains

Earl Richard's Great Hall is thought to stand on the site of a residence of a Dark-Age ruler. When Richard arrived, all that remained of these buildings was a large grassy hollow with shallow terraces and possibly the traces of tumbled walls about the area. Whether Richard valued this position because of its associations, or because it was easily defensible, he built on top of these remains a large, entirely new structure.

It was only in the 20th century that hundreds of pieces of fifth- to seventh-century pottery, animal bones and evidence of metalworking and building were discovered in a very small excavation, and these give tantalizing hints of what may lie buried under the 13th-century hall.

5 IRON GATE

On leaving the Great Hall the path immediately to the right leads down towards a cleft in the rocks, forming a small cove that faces north-east and is sheltered from the prevailing westerly winds. The

path stops before reaching the cove at an archway in a curtain wall, which was once closed off by a gate. From here defenders could prevent access to the land via the cove and the larger Haven to the south. John Leland, visiting the site in 1540, writes that 'men alyve saw ther yn a posterne dore of yren' and John Norden labelled this section of his map of 1604 'the Iron Gate'.

There is now no access to the cove beyond the curtain wall, which runs from the edge of the cliff overlooking the cove to a point about 30m to the south-east where the slope becomes precipitous. The wall seems to have been built at the same time as the castle, although it was later strengthened at its southern end by a thinner battlemented wall. It has a wall-walk protected by a battlemented parapet. The merlons (the raised teeth of the battlements) are pierced with arrow-slits.

In 1583, at the time of the threat of invasion from Spain before the Armada of 1588, the naval commander Sir Richard Grenville (1542–91) recorded the use of the Iron Gate as a landing place, noting that four or five ships could 'with most windes, ride, and lay their sides to the workes and land anie companie of men'. He saw the potential weakness of this spot and proposed two bulwarks or round gun platforms as additions to the Iron Gate. These appear to have been built, and one survived until 1817.

Below: Glass fragments found in the lower mainland courtyard at Tintagel (see page 6) came from a bowl decorated with an inscription similar to this one from Holme Pierrepont in Nottinghamshire
Bottom: The Island remains looking south towards the Island courtyard; to the left of the path are some of the Dark-Age remains

Dark-Age Remains

In the area around the Iron Gate many pieces of pottery have been found, some later medieval, but many more early medieval, dating from the fifth to the seventh centuries. It is likely that any imported goods from the Mediterranean that were brought to Tintagel by sea, rather than overland from a harbour on the south coast, were brought ashore here during this time. Buildings recently discovered running along the side of the pathway down to the gate may have been storehouses from this early period. They are located on ledges that are now concealed by scree collapse from the slope above.

The tour continues on the main path in front of the stone membership hut (where a handling collection of potsherds is sometimes available).

6 THE DARK-AGE REMAINS

Both on the sloping edges and on the flatter top of the Island are grass-covered foundations, most of which are now thought to have formed part of the extensive settlement that existed during the Dark Ages. Those that are visible across the headland are those that were reconstructed by Ralegh Radford's team in the 1930s. In the 1980s several small-scale excavations were carried out on the Island and the nearby mainland, mostly after chance discoveries through erosion and an extensive fire in 1983, which burnt off much of the surface turf on the Island to reveal buildings and debris beneath.

In 1990 a larger-scale excavation project was begun to investigate the buildings that Ralegh Radford had uncovered in the 1930s and to determine whether they were part of the 13th-century castle complex or from the Dark Ages. Although Radford had denied the possibility of earlier timber buildings on the Island, this is exactly what was discovered.

There are four main groups of grass-covered foundations along the sheltered sloping side of the Island facing the Haven. The walls of these buildings are too incomplete to work out the original plan, but the narrow terraces, perhaps enlarged by hacking away part of the rock face, suggest that they would have been simple, slightly squared and

irregularly shaped buildings set into the back of the quarried terrace, later replaced by insubstantial stone buildings with walls of thin slates and earth cores. These structures now appear to be open to the seas, but it is likely that there were once seaward walls, now lost down the steep slope.

The huts are unlike any other Dark-Age ruins found in Cornwall. They are rectangular, rather than the round or ovoid forms found at such sites as Trethurgy near St Austell. Until further excavations and investigations are carried out, it is difficult to estimate how many people lived and worked here, and whether they did so temporarily or were seasonal inhabitants. It is certain, however, that an extensive settlement of some sort existed here at Tintagel during the Dark Ages, leaving behind it masses of imported pottery from the fifth to the seventh centuries.

Finds Along the Steps

Beyond the stone membership hut are steps heading left up the hill towards the top of the Island and directly to the chapel. Excavations

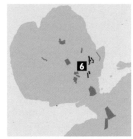

Left: Dark-Age remains overlooking the Haven. Earlier timber-framed buildings were replaced by these simple stone structures on the lower eastern slopes

Below: A reconstruction drawing of Tintagel as it may have looked in about 700, showing the Island dotted with simple houses

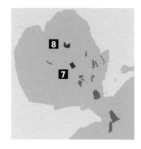

along the line of these steps revealed the site of Dark-Age rubbish dumps, containing large quantities of fragments of imported pottery from the Mediterranean.

In 2007, buildings believed to date from the Dark Ages were identified just in front of the hut. The sloping area on the right of the steps probably conceals shallow terraces on which buildings had been constructed. This can be seen more clearly further along the main path past the membership hut in the direction of the viewpoint.

Finds along the Pathway

The grass-covered walls to the left and right of the flat section of pathway towards the viewpoint were concealed by scree that had fallen from the slopes above, until Radford uncovered them, believing them to constitute a monastic scriptorium (a room set apart for the copying of manuscripts) (see page 19).

The complex on the lower side of the pathway is now thought to be Dark Age (although the group to the left of the path, just beyond the steps, dates from the time of the castle).

Higher up the eastern side of the Island, underneath the existing stone outlines of the rectangular building, the remains of an earlier timber phase (possibly fourth to fifth century) were discovered, marked out by post holes set into the bedrock and with clear floor layers. Similar remains were found on the upper part of the Island where the 1983 fire removed the overlying turf.

Viewing Platform

Excavations of the structures down the slope ahead of the viewing platform have shown that these buildings were relatively substantial and date from the Dark Ages. It was in this area that recent excavations uncovered not only ceramics from the Mediterranean, but also glass from Spain, and the celebrated 'Artognou slate'.

The earliest buildings in this part of the site were constructed in the fifth century. Made of wood with low stone walls, they hugged the narrow terrace of the lower slope and were flimsy, possibly occupied for only a few months each year. They may have served as store rooms or workshops. There is no evidence on this lower

Discovery of the Artognou Slate

Below: The Artognou slate, found on the eastern slopes of Tintagel Island. It had been trimmed to fit over a fifth- to seventh-century drain near the main buildings on the terrace

A piece of slate discovered in 1998 had two surviving sets of partial inscriptions. The first consists of four large letters and dates from before the second text. The second includes lightly inscribed letters that denote male personal names and is thought to date from the sixth century. All the lettering is in the nature of casual graffiti. As the stone is a fragment it is impossible to tell the intended meaning.

What remains of the second inscription is:

PATERN[I], COLIAVI FICIT
ARTOGNOV, COL[IAVI]

The name Artognou is Celtic and can be translated as 'bear-famous' or 'famous in a bear-like way'; the image of the bear was used in early poetry to represent heroic valour. 'Art' (later 'Arth') was a common element in personal names. The similarity to Arthur is, however, only partial, and was shared by many other names.

Coliavi and Patern[i] are forms of name denoting relationship, but with only a fragment remaining the type of relationship remains unclear. 'Ficit' means 'he made', a reference probably to the stone-cutter, rather than the sort of wording used on a public work.

It is possible, given the casual style of the markings and the repetitive nature of the words, that a stone-cutter, or two stone-cutters, were simply practising the art of inscription.

Left: The northern ruins, exposed by erosion and by a fire in the 1920s, were first excavated by Ralegh Radford in the 1930s

Below left: In the Middle Ages this rectangular plot was probably laid out as a garden, though its exposed position, distant from the castle, is puzzling

Below: Lovers in a garden, from a manuscript of c.1475. In some versions of the myth of Tristan and Yseult, the lovers meet in the walled orchard of King Mark's court at Tintagel, after Tristan signals to Yseult by dropping bark into a stream

slope of buildings from the era of the castle, and it may be that the terrace was already covered over by scree and was effectively invisible.

Scattered through the remains of all these buildings were broken pieces of amphorae (wine jars), plates, dishes and glass vessels, all brought to the site directly in ships from main ports from the Mediterranean, north Africa and Spain or overland via British ports (see page 27).

7 GARDEN

This small walled area was first recorded by John Leland in the 1540s. He called it 'a grownd quadrant walled as yt were a garden plot'. For Sir Richard Grenville in 1583, it was 'a garden walled'.

Radford's excavations of the garden in the mid-1930s showed evidence of deep soil defined by upright slabs, which may have marked beds for herbs and flowers. It may well have been laid out in the Middle Ages as a walled garden, although its presence on such an exposed spot on the top of the Island is puzzling.

It is also probable that the area served as a sheep fold in recent times; given the difficulty of maintaining a garden even temporarily on the

Island, this may indeed have been its function for most of its history. The walls were consolidated in the 1930s by Ralegh Radford.

8 NORTHERN RUINS

These buildings, which are now reduced to low, grass-covered walls, were among the first to be exposed by erosion, and by a fire in the late 1920s. They were excavated under the supervision of Ralegh Radford in the early 1930s. Their date and function remain uncertain. Some may date back to

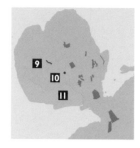

Right: The tunnel on the top of the Island. Its purpose remains unknown, though it may have been used for storage of some kind

Below: A kiln in the corner of one of the houses of the northern ruins. It was probably used for drying corn in the Middle Ages, when the Dark-Age buildings may have constituted a farmstead

the 1580s against possible Spanish attack at the suggestion of Sir Richard Grenville in the years before the arrival of the Spanish Armada.

9 TUNNEL

The origins of the tunnel are unknown. It may be an extension of a natural fissure enlarged by chiselling the rock – the marks made by a narrow chisel can be seen on the walls. John Leland saw it as 'the ruines of a vault', and other early visitors referred to it as a cave.

One idea is that it served as a long and narrow larder for the castle in the Middle Ages and may have had a door, set in a wooden frame, at the end nearer the sea to aid cooling and food preservation. There are suggestions of shelving supports or small cross-timbers in the interior. The tunnel is some distance from the Great Hall, however, and moving food to and from the tunnel to supply a castle that the earl and his retinue visited rarely, seems impractical.

10 WELL

The shallow depression on the top of the Island is the only natural water-catchment at Tintagel and several streams run from it. The present well, with its circular well-head, is assumed to date from the time of the castle. It would have been the main source of fresh water for the castle, apart from any water collected from the roofs of the buildings. An earlier well may have existed here during the Dark-Age occupation, although the earlier settlement probably made use of the natural spring on the eastern side of the headland.

Today the well is an essential part of the fire-fighting arrangements for the Island, in combination with a mechanical pump housed in a small stone structure nearby. This was built following the major fire of 1983, which devastated the vegetation on the upper part of the Island.

11 SOUTHERN CLIFFS

This part of the Island affords good views of the mainland, with the remains of the castle in the foreground and the parish church dedicated to St Materiana dominating the skyline. The church was built between about 1120 and 1140, replacing an early 11th-century building. A series of graves earlier than either of these buildings has been found in the churchyard. Some may date from

the fifth or sixth century (as seen on the eastern slopes of the Island) but others seem to be more recent. One, for example, has a small medieval-type corn-drying kiln at one corner and is presumed to have been seasonal in its use. The kiln is very similar to ones excavated in the medieval village at Houndtor on Dartmoor, which can be dated, and which would suggest that at least some of these buildings constituted a small homestead between the 10th and 12th centuries.

The small structure nearest the cliff edge may be the remains of a gun-house, erected in

Ralegh Radford and Tintagel

Courtenay Arthur Ralegh Radford was born in 1900 in Hillingdon, Middlesex, into a Devon-based family. After graduating from Oxford he helped excavate Whitby Abbey under Charles Peers, the Chief Inspector of Ancient Monuments. He then spent several years studying and travelling abroad. In 1933 he began excavations at Tintagel at the request of the Ministry of Works and in 1935 the first edition of his guide to the site was published.

Digging at the site was done by local workmen, under Radford's direction, and revealed the substantial remains of structures beyond the castle complex. Until the 1930s it was commonly accepted that Tintagel had been an early residence of King Arthur and of early Cornish rulers, but Radford concluded that the remains were those of a Celtic monastery, complete with scriptorium and monastic cells. The location of many of the trenches and what they revealed is known, though reconstruction of the remains often went unrecorded, which proves a challenge to modern archaeologists.

Radford also found many fragments of pottery, some of which were impressed with Christian symbols, and was the first to identify the fragments as imports from the Mediterranean of the late Roman world.

Between 1936 and 1939 Radford was director of the British School at Rome, spending the summers excavating back in Britain and in France. His involvement in excavations at Tintagel continued into the 1950s. He escaped from Italy just in time before the outbreak of the war. Few details are known of his war service but among other duties he served in the Secret Intelligence Service. In 1943 he became Chief Intelligence Officer in the Department of Psychological Warfare at Allied Headquarters in Algiers.

During the war he had little time to excavate, but from surviving correspondence it is clear he made brief visits to Tintagel. While excavating there he is said to have run up the steps from the bridge to the Island every morning. In 1942 his home in Exeter was bombed and many of the records of his work at Tintagel were destroyed.

Radford's view of Tintagel as a monastery held for more than 50 years, reinforced by his personal stature as an expert on early church archaeology

and fuelled by his worldwide travels to investigate the subject. But in the decades following his excavations re-examination of the evidence and new discoveries cast doubt on his interpretation.

Just before another series of excavations began in 1990, the 90-year-old Radford visited the site by helicopter. Though he had by then begun to question the reasons for the extensive trade of imported pottery found at the site, he never wavered in his belief that Tintagel was a monastic complex. He died on 27 December 1998.

'Arthur ... reigns supreme at Tintagel, and few would wish to displace him'

Above: Ralegh Radford in 1959, photographed by Walter Bird
Below: Ralegh Radford talking to visitors from amidst his excavations at Tintagel in the 1930s

the sixth century and may represent the Christian burials of the Island's occupants. The broad terrace below the viewpoint on the southern cliffs contains unexcavated buildings, probably Dark Age.

This area on top of the Island has large expanses of exposed bedrock. There seem to have been several buildings here and on the lower rock plateau to the east. Anyone erecting wooden buildings here would have had to dig into the rock and use the supporting stonework for the timber posts, as revealed in excavations elsewhere on the Island.

12 CHAPEL

The small chapel is dedicated to St Juliot, an obscure male Celtic saint. Around the outside of the ruined chapel are several fragments of grass-covered wall foundations – the remains of buildings of several dates, from the fifth to the seventh centuries and from the era of the castle. One of the earlier buildings seems to have been used as the foundations for the chapel. It was longer than other buildings on the site and had a roughly east-west axis and so may either have been a chapel during the days of the Dark-Age stronghold or have been adapted to form one.

Usually a chapel would have been built within the castle grounds. This chapel is some distance away, which suggests that it may pre-date the castle. A fine granite font similar to other fonts in the area and thought to date from the 11th century (now in Tintagel parish church on the mainland), and a stone carved with a rosette thought to date from the 12th or 13th century, also suggest an early date. But these stones may have been brought to the site from elsewhere, and if the early foundations upon which the chapel is built are the remains of a Dark-Age chapel, it is possible that the present chapel was built here for that reason at the same time as the castle.

The castle had its own chaplain who was obliged to live in the castle and perform offices regularly, for which, in the first half of the 14th century, he was paid 50s. a year. In 1388 a warrant was issued by Richard II to 'John Slegh, the King's Butler, Keeper of the King's Castle of Tyntagell, for the price of vestments of rich silk, of a red and blue colour … to be delivered to the same John in the said Castle for the use of a certain Chantry, for ever to be held within the said Castle'.

The chapel was still in use in 1483, when Richard III (r. 1483–5) appointed John Leicroft chaplain for the term of his life. It would have been a simple building: a wooden screen divided the nave, where the congregation stood, from

Above: *Granite stone found in the remains of the Island chapel and thought to date from the 12th or 13th century. It is now built into the side altar of the north transept of Tintagel parish church*
Left: *The remains of the chapel of St Juliot, with the Camelot Castle Hotel on the mainland in the distance*

Facing page: *View of Tintagel from the east, looking towards the Haven and Merlin's Cave*

Right: Mid-14th-century manuscript showing a priest wearing vestments of red and blue. Similar vestments were ordered by Richard II to be provided for the chaplain of Tintagel in 1388

Below: An 1842 engraving by W Finden, after J D Harding, showing the derricks and platforms from which slate was loaded onto ships in the Haven below

the chancel, where the altar lay on a raised step at the far end. The two holes just in front of the chancel probably mark the position of the screen. The original entrance to the chapel was in the south-west corner, but in the 13th century, when it was used by the occupants of the castle, it was blocked and another entrance inserted in the west end, probably protected by a small porch.

▣ ▤ THE HAVEN AND MERLIN'S CAVE

In descending to the Haven at the foot of the valley, the remains of the platforms and derricks via which slate was loaded onto the ships waiting in the harbour below can be seen on the right. An early 19th-century painting by J M W Turner shows workmen loading these derricks with the slate piled up around them on the platforms.

The Haven was long regarded as an excellent place to land. In 1583 Sir Richard Grenville surveyed the Island at a time of threat of Spanish invasion, noting that 'the greatest sortes of shippes … laye their sides to the workes and land and companie of men' at the Haven, and that it 'is all fayer sandy grounde good to ancor in and there is never lesse than five fathom of water at the loest ebbe, sheipes may ryed there all wyndes except the north west'. Photographs taken in the early 1900s show sailing ships in the Haven waiting to be loaded with slate.

On the west side of the Haven beach is the entrance to a cavern that passes right through the neck of the Island. It shows signs of having been widened as a consequence of mining work, but it has also been eroded by the water that runs through it at high tide. Since the late 19th century it has been named Merlin's Cave.

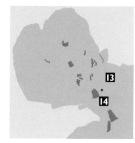

Above: Merlin's Cave as the rising sun catches the sea mist off the Haven
Left: Merlin stands on the shore of Tintagel as the sea delivers to him the future King Arthur in this illustration by Gustave Doré for a French edition (1868) of Idylls of the King, by Alfred, Lord Tennyson

Merlin's Cave is probably so-called because of the popularity of Tennyson's sequence of 12 poems, *Idylls of the King*, published between 1859 and 1885, in which Merlin plucks the infant Arthur from the sea:

> When Uther in Tintagil passed away
> Moaning and wailing for an heir ...
> the two [Merlin and Bleys]
> Dropt to the cove, and watched
>   the great sea fall,
> Wave after wave, each mightier than the last,
> Til last, a ninth one, gathering half the deep
> And full of voices, slowly rose and plunged
> Roaring, and all the wave was in a flame:
> And down the wave and in the flame was borne
> A naked babe, and rode to Merlin's feet,
> Who stoopt and caught the babe, and cried,
>   'The King!
>   Here is an heir for Uther!'

History of Tintagel

Tintagel has been inhabited at least since the late Roman period, and probably before. Between the fifth and seventh centuries AD, a prosperous community was based here. After a period of obscurity, Tintagel was named by Geoffrey of Monmouth in the 12th century as the place where the legendary King Arthur was conceived. This may have been what inspired Richard, earl of Cornwall, younger brother of Henry III, to build his castle here during the 1230s and 1240s. In the 1930s, the archaeologist Ralegh Radford proved through his discovery of pottery fragments that Tintagel was once part of a trading network that reached throughout the Mediterranean world. Radford thought that the earlier building remains here were those of a monastery, but it is now thought they belong to a much larger and earlier settlement, possibly a residence of local rulers.

Left: The numerous rocky headlands of the Cornish coast, seen here from the eastern slopes of Tintagel Island, provided easily defendable sites during the Iron Age

Below: Roman milestone, found in Tintagel parish churchyard and now in the church. It is inscribed IMPCG VAL LIC LICIN, which translates 'Emperor Caesar Galerius Valerius Licinianus Licinius'. Licinius reigned from AD 308 to 324

Facing page: King Mark discovers Tristan and Yseult embracing inside Tintagel Castle, and Tristan (on horseback) then leaves Tintagel in disgrace in this early 15th-century French manuscript

PRE-ROMAN TIMES

The coastline of this part of Cornwall is fretted with picturesque beaches and narrow bays that resound to crashing waves. Above are high rocky ridges that project like fingers into the sea. These promontories were ideal for defence as they could simply be cut off from the mainland by a deep ditch. Relatively easy to maintain, they provided a safe area for settlement above the seaways, secure from raiders by land.

Heavily defended headland settlements of this type are found in the Iron Age period (roughly seventh century BC to first century AD) and are common in Wales and Cornwall. There is one at Barras Nose to the immediate north of Tintagel, and another at Willapark near Boscastle; and although no conclusive evidence has been found that the Island was occupied in the Iron Age period, such an occupation remains possible.

The great ditch may well have had Iron-Age origins, although recent excavations have not produced any new dating evidence from before

the fifth to seventh centuries. Similarly, on the Island, later building has obliterated anything that may have remained from earlier stages of settlement. Iron-Age buildings are typically simple round structures, built of wood or stone, like those recently excavated at Trethurgy near St Austell, dating from between the second and sixth centuries.

There have been occasional stray finds of flint or quartz at the site of Tintagel, and, although both were used for making tools before the arrival of the Romans in Cornwall in the mid-first century, they may have continued to be used long afterwards and so can offer no certain proof of earlier settlement.

ROMAN AND NATIVE

The evidence for a Roman presence near Tintagel is slight and comes late in the Roman occupation of Britain (about AD 43–410). A Roman milestone from the third century was found in Tintagel churchyard in 1889 (it is now in the church) and

Above: A Roman trade ship is loaded with goods in this mosaic of the third to fourth centuries in the Villa Romana del Casale, Sicily

Below: A purse of Roman coins found near the great ditch included coins issued under the emperor Tetricus I (r.270–273/4), who is depicted here on a coin issued during his reign

another a few decades older was found and is still at Trethevy in the garden of a private house, 1.75 miles away. These two milestones, inscribed with the names of the current emperors, were markers on an officially signposted road running along the north Cornish coast.

Pottery from the third and fourth centuries has been found on both the east and west banks of the river Camel near Padstow, to the south-west of Tintagel, and it is known that rich tin resources in the area were exploited from the third century onwards. Roman forts, such as those recently discovered at Calstock churchyard, at Restormel and at Nanstallon near Bodmin, are in areas where tin or lead was extracted.

In the seventh century in northern Italy the Ravenna Cosmography was compiled. It listed towns in the Roman Empire using much earlier sources, and a town in the far south-west of Britain called Purocoronavis is named. This may be a corruption of a name 'Durocornovio' (not otherwise known), which would mean 'town of the Cornovii (the Cornish)'. It has been suggested that this name might have referred to Tintagel, but the

element 'Duro-' refers rather to a low-lying town, not a fortification, and there may be other sites in Cornwall that better match this meaning.

Archaeological evidence for the Roman period at Tintagel is limited. The insubstantial buildings supported by posts set into bedrock on the sheltered, eastern side of the Island and on the exposed areas of the top of the Island (see pages 14 and 16), were possibly temporary structures, for seasonal rather than year-round habitation, and would have been lived in by local people at the time of the Romans.

Small quantities of burnt oats, barley and wheat grains were discovered in recently excavated hearths dating from the late fourth to the mid-fifth centuries. Together with the presence of seeds from farmed land and the lack of chaff from the processing of the cereals, these findings raise the possibility that partially processed crops were brought to the Island. This evidence is matched at the mainland churchyard site. The presence of hazel charcoal may well indicate also that coppiced woodland in the vicinity was being exploited.

A chance find in 1955 of a small parcel of late fourth-century Roman coins in a crack in the side of the great ditch indicates contact with the Roman world; so too do fragments of Roman mortars and bowls from the third to fourth centuries, as well as locally produced Romano-British vessels. It is possible that these continued to be used – and perhaps even made – on the site as late as the fifth century. Some glass from these periods has also been discovered. Despite these discoveries, the evidence for Roman occupation at Tintagel remains too fragmentary for any definite conclusions to be reached about who lived here during the Roman period and how they worked or traded.

TINTAGEL AS PART OF THE MEDITERRANEAN WORLD

During the three centuries following the end of Roman administration in Britain in 410, population movements saw the creation of Anglo-Saxon kingdoms in south-eastern Britain. This period is often referred to as the Dark Ages, because so little is known about it, but archaeological investigations and discovery of imported pottery and extensive building remains show that between the fifth and seventh centuries Tintagel was the

Pottery Finds at Tintagel

Several thousand pieces of pottery have been found at Tintagel. Some are local Romano-British, and some are medieval and date from the time of the castle; but most date from the Dark Ages, and nearly all of the latter were imported from the Mediterranean.

In 1956 Ralegh Radford published an essay on the imported pottery so far uncovered at the site. The finds included fine red slip bowls and dishes (slip is a mixture of water and clay, with or without other finely ground minerals, used as a coating), amphorae (large, double-handled vessels for storing liquids), medieval jugs and pitchers, and some imported dark blue-grey slipware.

During the 1990s a further extensive collection of Mediterranean pottery dating from the fifth to the seventh centuries was found at Tintagel, and came to form the largest such collection in the British Isles. It includes about 150 storage jars of all types: one-metre high oil jars from north Africa (Tunisia), globular jars with short, conical necks from Greece, and jars with distinctive foot spikes, enabling them to stand without support, from Asia Minor. There were also finer pieces for use at table from western Turkey (Phocaea) and Tunisia (Carthage) and glass vessels, some originating from the Bordeaux region, and others from Carthage in north Africa, Cadiz in Spain, and from the East.

Nearly all the amphorae have two handles and all were used to transport commodities such as wine and olive oil. The jars would have been sealed with pottery discs that were used as lids once the jars reached their destination and had been opened. Sometimes discs of local stone are found; jars were evidently resealed after opening, and probably re-used once the original contents were consumed.

Despite the great quantity of imported pottery found, some local pottery was also used at Tintagel. It is likely that Tintagel itself was not a point of distribution for imported goods, but rather that ships from the Mediterranean brought cargoes to the south coast of Devon and Cornwall, exchanged their goods for British produce (such as tin), and from here the imports were distributed inland across Britain, to Tintagel and elsewhere.

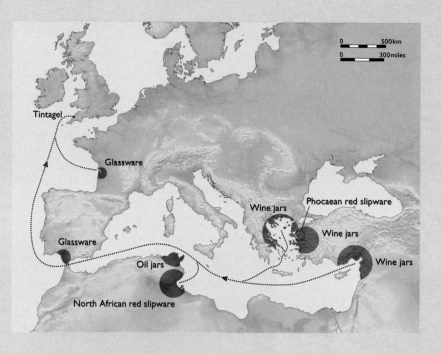

Oil jars from north Africa, globular jars from Greece, jars with foot spikes from Asia Minor, finer table pieces from western Turkey and glass from Bordeaux were all found at Tintagel

Above: At Tintagel pottery and glass were imported from all over the Mediterranean during the Dark Ages. The known sources of the wares are shown on this map
Left: Wine or oil jars (amphorae) of a type such as this one, from Pozzuoli in southern Italy, were imported to Tintagel

Right: *King Arthur battling a cat-like monster, known as the Chapalu, depicted in a floor mosaic in Otranto Cathedral, Italy, dating from between 1163 and 1166*

Below: *Arthur fighting the giant on St Michael's Mount, from an early 15th-century copy of Geoffrey of Monmouth's History of the Kings of Britain*

location of a substantial settlement that enjoyed commercial links with the Mediterranean.

Tintagel's importance within a trading network suggests that it may have been a fortress of the kings of Dumnonia, a post-Roman Celtic kingdom that included Cornwall, Devon and part of Somerset. Only two of Dumnonia's kings are known by name. One, Constantine, was labelled a murderer and an enemy of the Christian life by his contemporary the sixth-century Gildas, who is the only Dark-Age British writer to have provided any details of the people and events of that time.

Dumnonia survived until about AD 708–9, when the lands to the east of the river Tamar were annexed by the Anglo-Saxon kingdom of Wessex and Dumnonia's king, Gerent, was left ruling the reduced dominion to the west. The archaeological record at Tintagel falls almost silent in the seventh century. It is unclear why, but Tintagel seems to have been abandoned at this time. It is probable that contemporary political changes affected whatever administrative, trading or political function Tintagel had once had.

A sherd of glass from the eighth or ninth century and a coin of Alfred the Great (r.871–99) found in the 1930s in the area of the chapel on the top of the Island may well have been lost by isolated inhabitants or passing travellers.

THE EMERGENCE OF ARTHUR

The foremost figure popularly linked with Tintagel is King Arthur. There is minimal historical evidence for Arthur, and nothing to associate him with Tintagel until the 12th century. The earliest surviving mention of his name is in the *Historia Brittonum* (*History of the Britons*), a manuscript assembled from a mixture of historical sources and folk tales in north Wales about 829–30, attributed in one text to a scholar called Nennius.

The text presents two different versions of Arthur, one apparently based on historical fact – a Christian war leader who commanded the forces of 'the kings of the Britons' against the Saxons; and one more obviously mythical – a magical figure whose dog's paws made permanent impressions in stone, and whose son's tomb varied mysteriously: 'men come to measure the grave and find it sometimes six feet in length, sometimes nine, sometimes twelve, sometimes fifteen. At whatever length you might measure it at one time, a second time you will not find it to have the same length'.

Arthur was probably included in the *Historia Brittonum* to please Merfyn Frych, king of Gwynedd in north Wales. The first of a new dynasty of kings, Merfyn may have wanted to associate himself with a war hero believed to have repeatedly defeated the forebears of the English kings who harassed Wales in the early ninth century.

There is evidence that at about the same time Arthur, often linked with features in the landscape, was the subject of popular legend in Cornwall, southern Scotland and Brittany.

THE TALES OF GEOFFREY OF MONMOUTH

Arthur's enormous international popularity was largely owing to one author, a scholar called Geoffrey of Monmouth (d.1154/5). It was he who first linked Arthur with Tintagel, describing it as the island fortress where Arthur was conceived thanks to the magic of Merlin.

In about 1138, Geoffrey drastically embellished previous accounts of Arthur in his *Historia regum Britanniae* (*History of the Kings of Britain*). By this time, stories of Arthur and his warriors were already known on the Continent.

Geoffrey described Arthur as a 'youth of unparalleled courage and generosity, joined with that sweetness of temper and innate goodness, as gained him universal love' and turned him, as an adult, from a victorious battle leader into the greatest of a line of kings of Britain, and conqueror of most of western and northern Europe, whose renown had attracted the bravest knights of the Continent to his court. Geoffrey also included elements of legend that depicted Arthur defeating a giant on St Michael's Mount.

Despite these more obvious fantasies, Geoffrey placed Arthur in an apparently historical sixth-century Britain, expressed in detail relevant to his 12th-century audience, and so provided the court of the Norman kings of England with a credible heroic role model.

ARTHUR AND TINTAGEL

Tintagel enters the story of Arthur when Geoffrey tells how Uther Pendragon, king of Britain, fell in love with Igerna (Ygraine), wife of Gorlois, duke of Cornwall. Tintagel is presented as Gorlois's strongest fortress, where he placed Igerna to protect her from Uther's advances. While Uther's forces besiege Gorlois elsewhere in Cornwall, Uther's adviser, the wizard Merlin, transforms Uther into the likeness of Gorlois. Uther and his companion 'set forward on their way to Tintagel, at which they arrived in the evening twilight' and are admitted by the porter to the castle and to Igerna on the strength of their disguises. 'The same night

therefore she conceived of the most renowned Arthur, whose heroic and wonderful actions have justly rendered his name famous'. Gorlois is then killed in battle and Uther marries Igerna.

The river Camblan, the site of Arthur's last battle, was also placed by Geoffrey in Cornwall. It is highly likely, judging from Geoffrey's description of Tintagel, that he had visited Tintagel (or got a description from someone who had), and so knew of the great ditch, the ramparts, and the ruins of the buildings that had stood nearby when the site was heavily populated before the seventh century.

Left: Uther and Merlin arrive at Tintagel, and (in the lower panel) Uther is given access to the queen, Igerna, who is 'deceived with the false disguise which he had put on' and becomes pregnant with Arthur, in this 14th-century manuscript

Below: Arthur's last battle, shown in a 13th-century illustration, along the banks of the river Camblan, which Geoffrey of Monmouth placed in Cornwall. Here Arthur was fatally wounded by his kinsman Mordred

Knights, Chivalry, and Romance

Above: *Funeral badge of Edward, the Black Prince, in the form of a garter. Edward's father, Edward III, founded the chivalric Order of the Garter in about 1348*

Below: *The earliest known Arthurian Round Table, dating from about 1290 (the painting on the surface of the table top is 16th century). It now hangs in the Great Hall of Winchester Castle*

Stories of Arthur's court flourished in late 12th-century France, when the Plantagenet monarchs of England, Henry II (r.1154–89), his queen, Eleanor of Aquitaine, and their son, the future Richard I, controlled an arc of territory from Normandy to the Pyrenees.

In 1155, about 20 years after Geoffrey of Monmouth's *Historia*, Wace, an Anglo-Norman poet and courtier to Henry II, translated Geoffrey's work into Norman French. He added details of his own, such as the Round Table, where no knight had precedence over another.

The tales of the Knights of the Round Table became the pattern for a new order, a code of chivalry – the good conduct expected of a knight towards his enemies, his liege lord, his fellow knights, the lower orders, and women. It was the age, too, of the 'romance', a story in verse or prose placing a great emphasis on a knight's courtly and unfulfilled love for a lady, often the wife of his feudal superior or another lord.

The link between Arthur and his knights and the Holy Grail (the cup used by Christ at the Last Supper) was made in the early 13th century in the Vulgate Cycle, an early French source of Arthurian legend. It was later an important literary source for the English writer Sir Thomas Malory (c.1405–1471), and the image of noble knights engaged in this virtuous quest became a lasting part of the Arthurian myth.

English kings used the legend of King Arthur and the associated order of obedience and loyalty to promote their own political standing and ambitions. In the 12th century Henry II was said to have been involved in the discovery of a grave at Glastonbury thought to hold the remains of Arthur and Guinevere. His son Richard I presented a sword believed to be Excalibur to a foreign ruler.

It is thought by many that Richard of Cornwall's building of Tintagel Castle in the 1230s and 1240s was a realization of Arthurian fantasy. His brother Henry III wrote in 1232 of a type of tournament known as a 'round table' and his nephew Edward I (r.1272–1307) was said to have taken a book of Arthurian romance with him on crusade. During the rising opposition of the Welsh in 1278 Edward attended the reinterment of the supposed bones of Arthur and Guinevere at Glastonbury. It is possible he wanted to put to rest the myth cherished by the Welsh that Arthur would return to rule them.

In the 14th century the chivalric virtues, embodied by the legendary knights of Arthur's court, were adopted as the standards of conduct in institutions founded by the king. Edward III (r.1326/7–77) in 1344 proposed an Order of the Round Table, which, according to the English historian Adam Murimuth (d.1347), was to be established 'in the same manner and condition as Arthur, formerly king of England, established it'. The king's teenage son the Black Prince (1330–76), who had been made earl of Cornwall in 1336 and duke of Cornwall the following year, and with the titles held Tintagel Castle, was present on the occasion. A building was begun at Windsor Castle to house the Round Table, but the Order did not last.

Instead Edward, with the involvement of the Black Prince, founded another, similarly chivalric order, to consist of the king, the prince of Wales and 24 knights: the Order of the Garter, which remains today.

Left: An ivory casket made in France between 1325 and 1350, showing on the left Tristan and Yseult beneath a tree in which King Mark is hidden
Below left: King Mark confronts Yseult and Tristan over their unfaithfulness in this French manuscript of about 1470
Below: The sixth-century standing stone near Fowey, inscribed in Latin 'Here lies Drustanus, son of Cunomorus'. Some believe Drustanus to be Tristan

KING MARK OF CORNWALL

It should be remembered that Tintagel is hardly mentioned in Arthurian romance except in the work of Geoffrey and his followers. An educated European in about 1200 would sooner have associated the name Tintagel with the legendary figures of Mark and Tristan.

King Mark of Cornwall first appears as a local king in legends from Wales, Cornwall and Brittany. In his ninth-century *Life of St Paul Aurelian*, Wrmonoc, a Breton monk, identifies Mark with a King Cunomorus who ruled in Cornwall in the sixth century.

A standing stone near Fowey claims to mark the grave of Drustanus, son of Cunomorus. It has been suggested that Drustanus is Tristan, son of Mark. Ralegh Radford thought that Castle Dore, a small Iron Age fort near Fowey, had been Cunomorus's fortress but the fort is now known to have had no significant Dark-Age occupation.

The connection of the name Tristan with Tintagel arose in the 12th century, when the earliest surviving written accounts of the story of Tristan and Yseult – Continental poems from France and Germany – were first composed. In these Tintagel appears as the location of King Mark's court. Tristan is not his son, but his nephew, who becomes the lover of Mark's wife, Yseult.

It is unclear where the story originated. (There are early parallels with the Irish folktales of Diarmuid and Grainne, and the wooing of Emer, and a similar story exists in Persian literature.) There are several allusions to Tristan in medieval Welsh poetry, and these may pre-date the romances of the 12th century, or stem from a tradition uninfluenced by the Continental poems.

Though originally part of a separate story, by the end of the 12th century Mark, Tristan and Yseult had been drawn firmly into the ambit of Arthur – Mark as a contemporary minor king and Tristan as a Knight of the Round Table.

RICHARD, EARL OF CORNWALL

Arthur and his knights would have been the principal role models for boys in royal and noble households, including Richard (1209–72), second son of King John (r.1199–1216) and younger brother of Henry III (r.1216–72). He had huge estates in England, and used this wealth to pursue a European throne, but though he was crowned King of the Romans on 17 May 1257, making him notionally the king of Germany, he never managed to translate this title into real power there.

Richard was made earl of Cornwall by Henry in 1227, making him the most powerful man in the county. He visited Cornwall intermittently between 1229 and 1259; in the early 1230s he had to defend his rights as earl against the representatives of his brother the king.

Between about 1233 and 1236 Richard bought the headland and then the surrounding manor of Bossiney, whose name was later changed to Tintagel. By presenting himself as a worthy successor to King Arthur, Richard was asserting his royal status and his position within the county, in terms of local tradition.

Although Ralegh Radford thought that parts of the castle had been built in the 1140s by Reginald, a 12th-century earl of Cornwall and the illegitimate son of Henry I (r.1100–35), this is now considered unlikely. The scarcity of 12th-century pottery on the site suggests that the fabric of the castle is no older than Richard's time. What is more, during the

Knaresborough

Kirton-in-Lindsey ●

● Oakham

● Glatton

● Eye
● Haughley

Hailes Abbey ●   ● Watlington   ● Newport
        Ambrosden ●   ● Risborough
        Beckley ●
        Oxford ●   ● Berkhamsted
    Lechlade ●   ● Marlow
● Thornbury   Harwell ●
            Wallingford ┘   ● Iver
    ● Corsham   Benson ┘   Isleworth
                Henley ┘   └ Cippenham

        Mere ●   ● Wilton
        ● Ilchester

                    Chichester ●
    ┌ Launceston   ● Bradninch
    ┌ Lifton   ● Fordington
Tintagel ●   ● Exeter
Bodmin ┐   ┌ Liskeard   └ Lydford
Restormel ┘ ● Calstock
            ┘ Trematon
        ┌ West Looe
Helston ●
        └ Lostwithiel

● Holdings
● Holdings with castles

The Wealth of Richard of Cornwall

The construction of a castle at Tintagel would have done little to dent the wealth of one of the richest men in Europe. While many of Richard's surviving charters concern the boroughs of Cornwall, which was one of the major sources of his revenues, profiting as he did from the export of Cornish tin, he rarely visited the county.

After a violent quarrel at the age of 18 with his brother Henry III over his lack of land, Richard's loyalty to the king was steadfast. He was richly rewarded with landed estates during his lifetime and his second marriage, to Sanchia of Provence, brought him further wealth.

During the rebellion of the barons under Simon de Montfort against the king, Richard fought alongside his brother. At the battle of Lewes in 1264 he was captured, taken prisoner, and for some time he was held at Kenilworth. Even in defeat, he was kept in some luxury. His estates had been seized

by the victorious Simon de Montfort but Richard's sister Eleanor sent him presents of dates, ginger, cloves, almonds, raisins, pepper, and sugar, as well as wine, scarlet cloth for his robes, and hoods of satin and miniver. After the victory of the royalists at the battle of Evesham in 1265 Richard regained his estates, and was further rewarded with land confiscated from the defeated barons.

Richard founded several religious houses, notably Hailes Abbey, which he built in fulfilment of an oath. In 1242 he had narrowly escaped shipwreck during a storm, swearing to found an abbey if he survived. Sanchia was buried at Hailes in 1262. In 1271 Richard's oldest son, Henry of Almain, was murdered by his cousins the de Montforts, who had risen in opposition to the king, and buried at Hailes. Richard's death a year later was said to have been hastened by the shock of his son's. He was buried beside Sanchia and Henry in April 1272.

Above: Richard's principal holdings in about 1250. Although Cornwall was a major source of revenue, the earl's wealth and power extended far beyond its boundaries

Above left: Seal of Richard, earl of Cornwall, count of Poitou and king of the Romans

Above: Richard Carew, a 16th-century portrait of the English school
Right: Edward III granting his son, the Black Prince, the principality of Aquitaine, in a late 14th-century manuscript
Below: A jug dating from the time of Richard of Cornwall, found at Launceston Castle, where Richard spent Christmas in 1256

20 years of civil war that followed the death of Henry, Reginald would have had neither the leisure nor the motivation to build here. Lastly, there is no mention of Tintagel in any historical source until after 1200.

Richard's workforce used locally quarried slate and stone, the same as that used in the fifth to seventh centuries, and the castle was built over remains from these earlier periods. Little is known about the construction of the castle, in part because debris from its collapse was cleared when the site was being prepared to be opened to the public in the 1930s.

There is no record that Richard ever stayed at Tintagel – and if he did, it was not for long, though he spent Christmas at Launceston in 1256. A favourite residence of his in England was Beckley in Oxfordshire and he had major estates in Hertfordshire and other counties. He also spent long periods abroad, including that on crusade in the Holy Land in 1240–41 and on frequent visits to France. From 1256 he spent time in Germany, pursuing an attempt to make his disputed election as king of Germany effective, and then be crowned in Rome as Holy Roman Emperor.

According to the historian Matthew Paris (d. 1259), Richard granted his nephew Dafydd ap Llywelyn, son of his illegitimate sister Joan, asylum at Tintagel in 1245 while Dafydd was in rebellion against his uncle, Richard's brother Henry III.

Richard died in 1272 and the castle seems to have been kept up by his son Edmund, who died in 1300 without an heir. The earldom of Cornwall and its estates then returned to Edmund's cousin Edward I.

TINTAGEL AS A PRISON

After the death of Edmund in 1300 the castle was little used and fell into disrepair. By 1337 the roof of the Great Hall had been removed and put into store. The care of the castle passed through the hands of various non-resident stewards. The constable of Tintagel from 1351 until after 1364, John de Shirbec, let the land for grazing to the local vicar until the vicar's death. He then let it 'together with the profits of the rabbits there' to a local freeman.

Despite the castle's increasingly ruinous condition, Mass was still said in the chapel on the Island. A survey of the properties made in 1337 for

the Black Prince, son of Edward III, who became that year the first duke of Cornwall, described 'two decayed chambers over the two gateways, one sufficient chamber with a kitchen for the constable, a decayed stable for eight horses, a cellar, and a ruined bakehouse'. Grazing of sheep is recorded at this time, and continued into the 19th century.

In the 1350s, a new two-storey house was built within the walls of the Great Hall. It may have been part of a repair regime across Cornwall instigated by the Black Prince. By 1350 the Black Death had peaked across Europe; it must have affected the availability of chaplains, for although the usual chaplain's payment throughout the 13th century was 50s. a year, in 1356 Edward paid his chaplain at Trematon Castle, near Saltash in Cornwall, 66s. 8d., and nine months later the chaplain at Tintagel left 'on account of the smallness of his fee' of 50s. The constable was ordered to appoint a new chaplain and increase the fee to 66s. 8d.

In the 14th century, the castle was used as a prison, with state prisoners being despatched into the custody of the resident constable. In 1385 John Northampton, Lord Mayor of London, was, according to the Cornish antiquary and poet Richard Carew (1555–1620), 'for his unruly maioralty condemned thither as a perpetual penitenciary'. Thomas, earl of Warwick, was briefly a prisoner at Tintagel in 1397, having been transferred from the Tower of London on a trumped-up charge of treason. In 1386, Richard II (r.1377–99) ordered that Tintagel and Trematon Castle be surveyed and refortified against a possible French invasion.

THE CASTLE IN RUINS

By the later 15th century the castle was once more described as being in ruins. In 1540 John Leland, the antiquary, noted on his visit, 'the residew of the buildings of the castel be sore wetherbeten and in ruine (but it hath been a large thing)'. He also remarked that sheep were grazing within the castle walls, and provided the first mention of the garden: 'a grownd quadrant walled as yt were a garden plot'.

The garden was also shown on the plan made by Cornish landowner and sea captain Sir Richard Grenville, while conducting a survey in 1583 to see whether or not Tintagel and other fortresses needed to be strengthened in case of Spanish attack. It appears again on John Norden's drawing of about 1604 but without any annotation.

English interest in Arthur had again been stimulated in 1485 by William Caxton's publication of *Le Morte Darthur* by Sir Thomas Malory. This told the full story of Arthur in English, assembled from a variety of authorities, and again featured Tintagel prominently as the place of Arthur's conception.

The topographer William Worcester (b.1415) wrote about his visit to 'castrum de Tyntagelle' in 1478 and for the first time referred to it as the place of both Arthur's conception and his birth. As the 16th century progressed, Renaissance enthusiasm for rational enquiry in antiquarian study, and the depiction of idealized moral virtues in heroic literature, meant a waning of interest in Arthurian romance.

Despite Grenville's survey, the government of Elizabeth I had no official use for Tintagel, and on the death of the last constable, John Arundell, in 1597, the post was abolished.

An Arthurian poem of 1598, 'A Herryng's Tayle', probably written by Richard Carew, was set at Tintagel, but its hero was a snail: the fantastic world of the Arthurian legends was now a fit subject for ridicule.

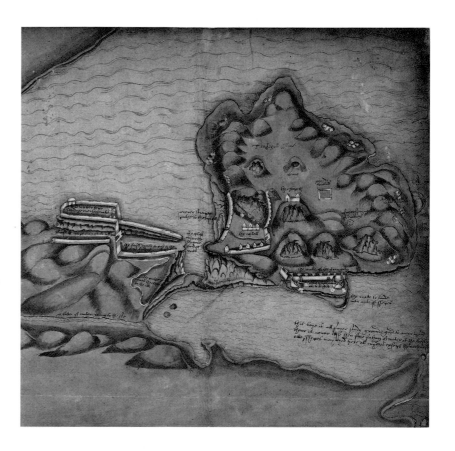

Above: *Sir Richard Grenville's plan of Tintagel, from his survey of 1583*
Left: *The naval commander Sir Richard Grenville in 1571, after an unknown artist. Grenville died of wounds fighting at sea in 1591. Tennyson, who celebrated Arthur in his Idylls of the King, also celebrated Grenville in his poem 'The Revenge'*

Above: Slate quarriers at Trevillet Quarry, Tintagel, in about 1930

Right: A ship in the Haven in about 1875, where it would have been loaded with slate at low tide. The entrance to the silver lead mine can be seen to the right of Merlin's Cave

THE FADING MYTH

Nevertheless, many details that were first supplied by Geoffrey of Monmouth or his successors were accepted as history by 17th-century antiquarians. On his 1604 drawing of the castle ruins, John Norden noted, 'The famous Arthure Kynge of the Brytons was here begotten in this castle'. The first large-scale map of Cornwall, published in 1699, marked 'King Arther's Castle', but by then interest in the Arthur of romance was at a low ebb. Early 18th-century antiquarians were engaged by more

ancient sites and those that were more easily accessible by coach roads from London, such as Avebury and Stonehenge. Tintagel Castle, lacking military, residential or decorative function, was an almost forgotten curiosity.

LIFE AND WORK AT TINTAGEL

By the 17th century, life at Tintagel Castle was overshadowed by the local industries of agriculture and slate quarrying. The latter dominated the lives of local inhabitants: the quarry at Delabole is recorded in the Elizabethan era, and no fewer than 21 quarries were active in 1650 in the sea cliffs on either side of Tintagel. It is likely that slate was being quarried as early as the Roman period, as indicated by the presence at Tintagel of inscribed slates, including that with the Artognou inscription. The massive extraction that took place over the centuries from the cliffs around Tintagel and Trebarwith was labour-intensive. The stone was hewn by hand, lowered by ropes, split into slates and then transported by sea. Vessels in the Haven at Tintagel would have been loaded as quickly as possible at low tide, leaving the inlet when the waves rose.

Mining in the area of Tintagel has a long history. Chief among the minerals mined was copper, extracted from inside Merlin's Cave. The major

resource of Cornish tin was an early export, probably from the Roman period onwards. Tin exportation was no doubt a major part of the trade with the Mediterranean that took place between the fifth and seventh centuries.

The mining of silver and lead took place in the 19th century and a mine gallery was driven under the Island in the 1870s. The present English Heritage café was built between 1870 and 1893 and was originally an equipment store and offices for the mine.

THE RETURN OF THE KING

There is no text, historical, romantic or any other, which presents Arthur as based at Tintagel in his career as king and leader. However, his association with Tintagel is indelible.

The late 18th and early 19th centuries brought a fascination with medievalism, seen in Gothic Revivalist architecture and the Gothic novels of the time. In 1816 Malory's *Le Morte Darthur* was reissued for the first time since 1634. In 1804 Sir Walter Scott had produced a new edition of the Middle Scots poem *Sir Tristrem* and renewed for a modern audience the love story of Tristan and Yseult. Tristan had since at least the 13th century been established in the Arthurian legend as a Knight of the Round Table.

Subsequent writers on Arthurian themes who made Tintagel prominent in their work included Alfred, Lord Tennyson (*Idylls of the King*, 1859–85) and Thomas Hardy in his *Famous Tragedy of the Queen of Cornwall* (1923). Robert Stephen Hawker (1803–75), vicar from 1834 of Morwenstow, about 20 miles north-east of Tintagel, wrote in 1863 the extremely popular poem *The Quest of the Sangraal*.

REVIVAL OF TINTAGEL

The renewed literary vogue for Arthurian matters was encouraged in the village of Tintagel by Richard Byrn Kinsman, vicar of Tintagel from 1851 to 1894. Kinsman was the son of a Cornish officer in the revenue service, and was educated in Cornwall before going to Trinity College, Cambridge, in 1830. Ordained priest in 1835, he served the entirety of his clerical career in Cornwall or Devon.

On taking over the parish of Tintagel he seems to have turned his attention at once to the castle

Left: Richard Byrn Kinsman, vicar of Tintagel parish from 1851 to 1894, who managed to obtain from Prince Albert the long-obsolete post of constable of Tintagel Castle
Below: *Detail of* The Last Sleep of Arthur in Avalon, *by Edward Burne-Jones, 1881–98. The mortally wounded Arthur is depicted in a trance-like sleep from which 'some men say' he will rise, as Malory writes in his* Morte Darthur, *'for King Arthur is not dead'*

Above: Florence Nightingale Richards at Tintagel, where she was self-appointed guide from childhood until she was 82

Above right: Florence Nightingale Richards's cottage, on the right of the track; it is now the site of the English Heritage shop and Visitor Centre. The buildings on the left now form the café

Below: An early postcard of King Arthur's Castle Hotel (later renamed the Camelot Castle Hotel)

ruins. He partly restored the battlemented wall on the mainland courtyard and the wall facing the mainland on the Island courtyard, and had steps carved into the cliff between them (these are now superseded in part by others).

Kinsman also successfully obtained from Prince Albert (husband of Queen Victoria), who acted as head of the duchy of Cornwall estate, the long-obsolete post of constable of Tintagel Castle, in recognition of his work on the site. He often acted as guide, showing visitors around the ruins himself with the assistance of Edwin Richards, who kept the key of the castle. Richards lived at the old mill in the valley between the castle and the village, and his daughter, the eccentric Florence Nightingale Richards (b. 1857), took over the keeping of the key from her father as a teenager, and continued to show visitors the remains of the castle until she was in her eighties.

Until about 1900, the name 'Tintagel' referred to the castle site and to the large surrounding parish, which encompassed a number of villages or hamlets. At about that time the nearest village to the castle, Trevena, also adopted the name 'Tintagel', so today this famous name refers to the castle, to the nearby village, and to the wider parish.

TOURISM

The renaming of this 'picturesque but straggling hamlet', as described in William Taylor's *History of Tintagel* in 1927, helped the village profit from the renewed popularity of Arthur in the 19th century and an expanding tourist trade. Writing on the Cornish coast in 1910, Charles G Harper described the significant impact of tourism in slightly grumbling tones: 'If it be rainy weather, the touring cars and the waggonettes churn up a fearful mud … Tennyson is responsible for this, for King Arthur and Tintagel had not become a cult before he wrote the *Idylls of the King*.'